Little Owl in the Big City

Little Owl in the Big City

Marcia Mogelonsky
Illustrated by Jill Alexander

Paulist Press
New York / Mahwah, NJ

Cover and interior art by Jill Alexander
Book design by Lynn Else

Library of Congress Control Number: 2021937982

ISBN 978-0-8091-6800-2 (hardcover)
ISBN 978-1-58768-983-3 (e-book)

Published by Paulist Press
997 Macarthur Boulevard
Mahwah, New Jersey 07430
www.paulistpress.com

Printed and bound in the
United States of America

by Corporate Graphics Commercial
North Mankato, MN
August 2021

For my dear husband Barry, who believed in Little Owl from the beginning.
—Marcia

My illustrations are affectionately dedicated to my mother, Carol.
Her unwavering support, sacrifices, and love led my dreams to take flight.
—Jill

About the Story

This is based on the true story of a Northern Saw-Whet owl found in the boughs of the Christmas tree at Rockefeller Center in 2020. The tree came from Oneonta, New York, 175 miles away. After being cared for at a wildlife center, the owl was released in a conifer forest in Upstate New York.

The Northern Saw-Whet is one of the smallest owls in the United States. It is famous for its nomadic ways; at nesting time, females take care of the eggs while males keep the family well-supplied with food, usually mice and other small rodents. But except for nesting periods, males tend to roam instead of staying in just one place.

THE BIG CITY TIMES

Tiny owl found in Rockefeller Center Christmas Tree

Did you see the newspaper?

There was a story about *ME!*

That was the big news... They "found me" in the tree.

Found me!

Found me?

But I was never lost.

I wanted to be in the tree.

Because I wanted to be in the Big City...

I wanted to see the tall buildings

And the lights

And hear the sounds of the people talking

And yelling

And singing

And the noises of the cars and the buses and the taxis.

I wanted to be in the middle of all the excitement and the noise and the lights.

You see, I am from a small town

Upstate

It doesn't have a lot of people

Or tall buildings

Or cars or buses or taxis.

It has small buildings and a few cars and buses...

And maybe a taxi or two.

It doesn't have bright lights

Or big noises

It is pretty

And quiet and dark and peaceful

But it is not exciting.

That tree...it is the Chosen Tree

Chosen to light up the Big City at Christmas.

It is a special tree.

Every year, a crew comes from the Big City to measure it

To see if it is tall enough to stand beside the tall buildings

And strong enough to hold the lights and the decorations

And big enough to carry the dreams of Christmas

For everyone who comes to see it.

When the crew came this fall

The robins heard them say "It's *TIME!*"

Time to bring the tree to the Big City for Christmas.

The robins told the chickadees

And the chickadees told the sparrows

And the sparrows told the squirrels

And everyone knows *they* can't keep quiet.

That's how I found out.

So, I packed my tiny bag

With a couple of tiny snacks

And I burrowed deep into the branches of the

Special Tree

And I waited.

And one morning some people came

And they wrapped the tree very carefully.

It was very warm and snuggly!

And away we went...

Onto the highway and into the Big City.

What a fun ride!

When we got there

They unwrapped the tree

And folded up the blankets.

They fluffed out the branches

And...

There was the city!

And the lights!

And the people!

And the buildings!

And the noise!

I wasn't lost

Even though the newspapers said I was *found*.

I got to the Big City

And that is where I wanted to be.

And I could see the tall buildings

And hear the noises

And watch the people hurrying everywhere

Talking and yelling and singing.

And as I sat on the tippy top branch

Of the Special Tree

Watching the people

And the buildings

And the lights

And the cars and buses and taxis

I was happy and grateful and so, so lucky!

And after sitting on the tippy top branch

Of the Special Tree

For a few days

I knew it was time to go home.

To my quiet town

With its tiny houses

And just a few buses and cars

And a taxi or two.

So I packed up my teeny tiny bag

And picked up some gifts to bring home to my friends:

Some worms for the robins

And some seeds for the chickadees

And even some nuts for the chattery squirrels

Because you know they would all be sad

If they didn't get a present.

And off I went.

Home

To the tiny town

And the little trees

And all my friends.

I liked my trip to the Big City...

But I am glad to be home

For now, anyway.